Surrendering it All
Writings from the heart

Regina Thrasher

Scripture quotations are taken from the Holy Bible, New Living Translation, copyright ©1996, 2004, 2015 by Tyndale House Foundation. Used by permission of Tyndale House Publishers, a Division of Tyndale House Ministries, Carol Stream, Illinois 60188. All rights reserved.

Copyrighted Material

Surrendering it All

Copyright ©2020 by Regina Thrasher.. All Rights Reserved.

No part of this publication may be reproduced, stored in a retrieval system or transmitted, in any form or by any means - electronic, mechanical, photocopying, recording or otherwise - without prior written permission from the publisher, except for the inclusion of brief quotations in a review.

For information about this title or to order other books and/or electronic media, contact the publisher:

ISBNs for Surrendering it All
Softcover: 978-1-732329-10-2
eBook: 978-1-732329-11-9

Printed in the United States of America

Cover Illustrator Joel Dunn:

DEDICATION

I am so humbled God has allowed me to write this book.
I couldn't have done it without my family & friends and their support.
You all inspire me daily to be a better wife, mother and daughter of the King
and I dedicate this book to God and my family with Love.

CONTENTS

Chains 3
Struggles 9
Label of Depression 17
Temptation 23
Going through the Motions 25
The Missing Piece 33
Pride 37
Sleeping Child 41
Years of my Life 47
Hate 53
Hearts Desire 59
Scars 65
"Family" 71
Giving Up 77
Pain 83
Faith 91
Surrendering it All 95

ACKNOWLEDGMENTS

There are way too many people that have encouraged me over the years to list them all here. My first and foremost goes to God whom laid on my heart to write this book and continues to show me Grace every day when I fail him. Thank you to my amazing family and friends that have lifted me up in prayer and life when I've needed it most. Thank you so much to Joel Dunn who is the young man that took my vision and created the illustration on the cover of this book from his heart. Lastly to the people that are reading this book, Thank you for your support and I pray it may in some way give you what you need today. God Bless you!

Foreword

It wouldn't be right if I didn't give you glimpse into the journey that God took me on, to get this book into your hands today. I will start from 5 years ago even though I know that God had been laying the groundwork my entire life.

Five years ago I married Michael and we blended our family of 5, even though this blended family had been living together for several years prior. We had both lost our mothers within 1 week the year before, and then I was laid off from a career that I had for over 25 years. I had started to hear the whispering from God in my head just a few short weeks before our wedding in August that he wanted me to write a book. Then I felt the biggest pull into a strange direction. You see I have always believed in God, and have heard from him on a few occasions the last couple years, so I tend to listen from experience, but I had never felt him drawing me towards something so strongly before. I have written my entire life, to many it is poetry, to me its always been about writing about something that was placed on my heart at the time. So the idea of writing a book wasn't completely a foreign thought, but that's not exactly what God told me. Here is what I heard. "Call your friends, Steve and Debbie, and asked them to go to their Condo with them in Port Aransas in September, and write."

I had a lot of questions about this for God. That means you want me to leave My new husband and 3 kids for a week just a few weeks after our honeymoon…What? Also, maybe even though Steve and Debbie are my best friends, maybe they don't want me to go on THEIR vacation? Every time I would question God, he just simply said… Go!

I dreaded what Michael would say even though he has seen God tell me a few things before. Our kids hate when God does that, by the way! I guess I shouldn't have been surprised when I told Michael about what God said and his response was, "Well I guess you need to go then". God had already prepared him. Now to make that phone call to Debbie. After she asked me some of the same questions that I had asked God, and discussed it with Steve they both emphatically said Yes. They had been going to this same condo for 20 years and only had a few guest over that time period, so they always enjoyed company.

Michael and I said our vows and went off to our honeymoon. I must tell you all honestly when you have 3 very demanding kids, teens and pre-teens, that I questioned God again why I had to leave the Bahamas and return home so soon to all that responsibility.

When I left for Port Aransas that week, the book you are reading is not what I was going to write. I was set on trying my hand at writing a fiction novel. I started the first morning we were there. In order for me to have some quiet writing time Steve went with Debbie on her morning walk on the beach each day. Something he had never done before in the past 20 years. I wrote a chapter a day for the first 4 day's. God was giving me the words to write each day. It was on that 4th day that Steve got up and walked into the bathroom and we heard a horrible noise. Steve had a heart attack and even though I tried my hardest to breathe life back into him, God had already called him home. It was then I had understood why I was supposed to be there that week, otherwise Debbie would have been there alone when she lost her husband of 35 years.

It took me almost a whole year before I started writing again. By this time, I knew that God was calling me more into the life of Woman's ministry and I had started doing more in this area. God then placed on my heart to write what you are reading now. I have discovered through this journey that we are all broken and cannot be fully mended unless we have a relationship with God. My prayer for anyone reading this is, if one thing that you read helps you where you are today in your journey towards a right relationship with our creator, press into it. If one thing you read helps you to realize that you are not alone, and you can endure anything, then writing this book was completely worth every second.

Chains

*We can rejoice, too, when we run into problems and trials,
for we know that they help us develop endurance.
And endurance develops strength of character,
and character strengthens our confident hope of salvation.
And this hope will not lead to disappointment.
For we know how dearly God loves us,
because he has given us the Holy Spirit to fill our hearts with his love.
When we were utterly helpless,
Christ came at just the right time and died for us sinners.*

Romans 5:3-6

Chains

How do you deal,
When you've lost your way?
You've given up hope,
And you struggle each day.

You search for an answer
You know you won't find
You look in all directions
But you're living a lie

On the outside your tough
On the inside you're scared
You look in the mirror
And don't like what's there

In a way you're glad
No one can see your soul
Because inside your dying
From that big black hole

That hole has been forged
By great suffering and pain
You feel like a prisoner
Held captive by chains

And then one day
You reach out in despair
You fall to your knees
And wonder if He cares

Would He talk to me,
So tainted with sin?
Would he open His arms,
And let me run in?

Or would he turn his back,
And just walk away?
Or would he really stop and listen
When I bowed to pray?

What did I have to lose
The chains gripped me so tight
If I handed Him my demons
Would he give me the strength to fight?

I looked towards the heavens
Said Father "I can't take any more,"
"I feel like I'm drowning,
I need to be restored"

All at once those chains
Dropped to the ground
I walk from the haze
And start looking around

Something was different
I felt lighter it seemed
Was I no longer alone,
Or is it all just a dream

Now each time I wake
I get stronger each day
As soon as I open my eyes
I begin to pray

Now when I look in the mirror
There's something different I see
You might call me crazy
It's God's image in me

It's like I have new eyes
That can see into my soul
Where once that void was
God has now made it whole.

Struggles

When you go through deep waters,
I will be with you.
When you go through rivers of difficulty,
you will not drown.
When you walk through the fire of oppression,
you will not be burned up;
the flames will not consume you.
For I am the Lord, your God,
the Holy One of Israel, your Savior.
I gave Egypt as a ransom for your freedom;
I gave Ethiopia and Seba in your place.
Others were given in exchange for you.
I traded their lives for yours
because you are precious to me.
You are honored, and I love you.
Isaiah 43:2-4

Struggles

Just when things get calm
And life is settling down again
Life throws another punch
Knocks you into a tail spin

How can things happen so fast
When you just made it through your last trouble
Sometimes it's just little things
Sometimes they're not so subtle

Little things seem to remind us
Not to take too much for granted
But the big things when they hit us
Can leave you lost and empty handed

Did I do something wrong
Or did I just somehow lose focus
Life is spiraling out of control
Leaving me feeling so hopeless

I know I have no power
I'm not the one in control
But that doesn't make it easier
I should be able to handle it on my own

God didn't put me in this position
If I call upon His name, He won't leave me there
But Satan is holding me down
Causing me to struggle and grasp for air

It will take every ounce of energy
To fight the enemy off of me
I have faith in His promises
To have a chance of breaking free

There is one thing I must remember
Keep it in the forefront of my mind
Nothing I will ever have to go through
Will be as hard as hanging on a cross, to die

So when I remember how He struggled
Hanging from nails that pierced His hands
Life struggles become in perspective
Glory is in God's plans.

Label of Depression

I waited patiently for the Lord to help me,
and he turned to me and heard my cry.
He lifted me out of the pit of despair,
out of the mud and the mire.
He set my feet on solid ground
and steadied me as I walked along.
He has given me a new song to sing,
a hymn of praise to our God.
Many will see what he has done and be amazed.
They will put their trust in the Lord.
Psalms 40:1-3

Label of Depression

There are these periods in my life
When my heart is full of pain
Not the physical kind you see,
That any doctor could explain

It's during these times
I just feel so dang sad
About nothing in particular
I just feel really bad

My eyes seems to glaze over
I feel dazed and confused
My body is throbbing with aches
Like I've been badly beaten and bruised

I try to contemplate the positive
All the things I'm grateful for
I have a roof over my head, a job,
And a loving family I adore

It's not that I don't appreciate
Please don't understand me wrong
It's just when it seems to happen
It's a grip that's way to strong

I hear this feeling has a name
Been labeled by the health profession
They will talk to you and give you a pill
Mark your chart with clinical depression

To be stuck with that label
It's a hard slap in my face
How could this happen to me,
When I'm covered by God's grace?

You see I AM a believer
I read God's word and go to church
But the deceiver is so good you see
He's been busy doing his research

He's been following me all around
Waiting to catch me when I'm weak
Then he whispers to me in my slumber
A perfect opportunity for him to speak

He knows I have the weapon to fight,
In God's word on the bedside table
That makes him work twice as hard
So when I wake I'll be unable

It's in these periods of my life
When I wake feeling this way
I have to hit the floor with my knees
And ceaselessly begin to pray

The feeling doesn't always leave
As fast as I would like it too
It may just hang around for a while
But with God I'll make it through.

Temptation

And remember, when you are being tempted, do not say, "God is tempting me." God is never tempted to do wrong, and he never tempts anyone else.
Temptation comes from our own desires, which entice us and drag us away. These desires give birth to sinful actions.
And when sin is allowed to grow, it gives birth to death.
So don't be misled, my dear brothers and sisters.
Whatever is good and perfect is a gift coming down to us from God our Father, who created all the lights in the heavens.
He never changes or casts a shifting shadow.
He chose to give birth to us by giving us his true word.
And we, out of all creation, became his prized possession.
James 1:13-18

Temptation

They say that Satan, is roaming around
You stay on the move, not wanting to be found
Some days it seems, you can't run fast enough
He catches you, and then things get rough

He whispers things that sound so true
He knows your weakness; he's been watching you
He uses temptation, makes you think it's right
Then he drowns you in darkness, no room for light

He stays happy, if he can keep you there
He wants you to think that no one else cares
He wants you to turn from everyone you knew
He'll help you build the walls they can't break through

You'll make him nervous if you question him
But he'll convince you what you're doing, is not sin
How can it be bad, when it feels so good?
To do what you want and not what you should

A stirring from my conscious, keeps on creeping in
Something I may have read, way back when
A passage about a lion, looking to devour
Could it have been to the evil one, I handed my power?

My eyes soon well up, my heart cries in pain
What have I done, I feel so ashamed
Could God forgive me, when I turned from his grace?
How could I have let Satan come in, and take His place?

"My Father, My Father, forgive me I plead
It was then I felt the warmth of His mighty arms around me
How did the deceiver make me believe he was right?
But I knew the answer, even God's children lose sight.

This world is filled with many temptations you see
That's why Jesus had to die on the cross, for us to be free!!

Going Through the Motions

*NEVER HAS MY HEART KNOWN A SWEETER
SOUL THAN MY BELOVED MOTHER*

*NORMA J. BECKHAM
AUGUST 11, 1937
AUGUST 7, 2014*

Going through the Motions

Each day I go through the motions
Not really knowing how or why
Struggling to move things forward
But all I want to do is cry

My heart has become so heavy
The pressure, it causes me to gasp for air
Some days I feel I'm drowning
Other days I struggle to care

Every time something good happens
It soon becomes cloudy and grey
Because the first person I wanna call and tell
Is now buried in a grave

I know she is in heaven watching
But it is just not the same
Oh Lord, I miss my momma
Please rid me of this pain

I know that time will heal my heart
It will get easier every day
I sure wish that knowledge would help me now
As I struggle to find my way

Trying to be strong sometimes is pointless
The tears keep streaking down my face
Every day there are more reminders
Of God's new Angel, that I can't replace

I know that I will get through this
This is just a fact of life
I just wish it would get easier
Not cause me so much strife

So now each day I will still go through the motions
Still not knowing how or why
Praying to God to help me move forward
Even though all I still wanna do, is cry!!!!

The Missing Piece

Therefore, put on every piece of God's armor so you will be able to resist the enemy in the time of evil.
Then after the battle you will still be standing firm.
Stand your ground, putting on the belt of truth and the body armor of God's righteousness.
For shoes, put on the peace that comes from the Good News so that you will be fully prepared.
In addition to all of these, hold up the shield of faith to stop the fiery arrows of the devil.
Put on salvation as your helmet, and take the sword of the Spirit, which is the word of God.
Pray in the Spirit at all times and on every occasion.
Stay alert and be persistent in your prayers for all believers everywhere.
Ephesians 6:13-18

The Missing Piece

Do you ever wake up lonely?
Or full of desperation and despair?
You can't seem to find any peace
And some days you struggle to even care

You seem to spend your days searching
Chasing people or things to fulfill that void
But nothing ever seems to make you happy
Your self-esteem has been destroyed

Each failure in life has taught you
Some valuable, but hard lessons
Satan wants you to believe you're not good enough
So you miss out on all God's real blessings

You see, Satan's job is to confuse you
He whispers lies into your mind
He makes you feel like a piece of you is missing
Pieces this world can only provide

These lies they can penetrate you
Sinking deep down into your soul
These lies they are meant to deceive you
They will take your life and spin it out of control

If Satan can just make you believe
That this world, can fulfill your hearts desires
Then he can keep you chasing in circles
And adding souls to his eternal fire

You may even reach this bad place
Several times throughout your life
Trust me, Satan he is a watching
Waiting to pounce when there is strife

On these days you must cling to God's promises
Hold them steadfast in your heart
Put on the armor God has provided
The armor, no man nor Satan, can ever rip apart

Facing the enemy sure is scary
Especially when you don't have the confidence to fight
But even Satan knows the power of God's mighty sword
Pick it up, watch the enemy tremble at its sight

You see, you are not a strong enough person
Not one who can defeat the enemy on our own
But by just inviting God inside of you
Then never again will you be alone

That doesn't mean that your future will be easy
You will have to make the choice every single day
But it does mean that your searching is over
He fills that void as he starts to mold you, like a beautiful,
precious piece of clay

Pride

"People cry out when they are oppressed.
They groan beneath the power of the mighty.
Yet they don't ask, 'Where is God my Creator,
the one who gives songs in the night?
Where is the one who makes us smarter than the animals
and wiser than the birds of the sky?'
And when they cry out, God does not answer
because of their pride.
But it is wrong to say God doesn't listen,
to say the Almighty isn't concerned.
You say you can't see him,
but he will bring justice if you will only wait.
You say he does not respond to sinners with anger
and is not greatly concerned about wickedness."
Job 35:9-15

Pride

What does the Bible say, God hates the most?
What is that thing within us, that makes us boast?
What is that voice that tells us, we don't need God on our side?
The Bible tells us my friend, that thing is pride!

Pride is that thing that starts deep within
It clouds your vision, and YES it is a sin
It will get in your head when you try to think things through
It will convince you of things that are completely untrue!

Pride is a tool that has been used through the ages
It will creep in slow and take you through many stages
It can start with a whisper, your better than them
And the next thing you know, you've hurt your best friend

Pride will tell you, only take care of yourself
Then soon that Bible will be collecting dust on the shelf
I can see why God hates this most deadly sin
It makes you think you're in control, and you don't need Him!

If pride has taken you down this dangerous road
Then you have some things in your heart you need to unload
Forget all the things pride has convinced you to be true
And turn to the One who is waiting for you!

Sleeping Child

*Direct your children onto the right path,
and when they are older, they will not leave it.*
Proverbs 22:6

Sleeping Child

When you're asleep
You look so sweet
I watch your lil' face
And it makes my heart break

I know the days
Will fly quickly by
And you'll be grown
In just a blink of an eye

You learn to crawl
And take your first step
And when you fall
There won't be a net

When you climb up on that bus,
And it takes you away
You'll head off to school
To start your first day
I'll feel so empty
Way down inside,
So don't be ashamed
When I stand there and cry

As years go by
You'll ask to go on a date
And I'll be worried sick
If he brings you home late

Then some day
A man will ask for your hand
And I'll cry once again
As you exchange those gold bands

Then one glorious day
You'll have your first child
You'll wonder as I look at you,
Why do I smile

My mind wanders back
To when I watched you sleep
Alone in your dreams
As I quietly creeped

I say a silent prayer
To God our creator
Cause the best gift He gave me
Is the day that He made her.

Years of my Life

*"But forget all that—
it is nothing compared to what I am going to do.
For I am about to do something new.
See, I have already begun! Do you not see it?
I will make a pathway through the wilderness.
I will create rivers in the dry wasteland."
Isaiah 43:18-19*

Years of my Life

The years haven't always been too kind
Some days, I wish I could rewind
Others you want to fast forward
Some I couldn't imagine having to do over

As I look back, there are things I would change
Make the results not quite the same
But would that change who I became?
Make me a better person, or drive me insane?

I have always been strong for a reason
God made me that way to weather all seasons
But sometimes it's hard when I look inside
I am not quite sure I am enjoying the ride

There are deep dark valleys in life
And they can cause you great heartache and strife
You long to find the light that's up ahead
But some days it's a struggle just to get out of bed

But when you're on the mountain top looking down
It's not hard to see, the beauty that's all around
You see we were created for God's own plan
It's on that mountain we can see where he has placed his hand

See always staying on that mountain, just wouldn't be right
We need the valleys of darkness, to see God's pure light
When you're up on top, you look down away from his face
But when you're on bottom, you look up and search for his Grace

He molded me in His image, then left me that way
Then gave me free will, and waited till I prayed
I had to invite Him in, he wouldn't force himself there
He watched and He waited until I realized He cared

We do that with our children,
Don't want them to make mistakes
We send them out on their own
In a world full of heart breaks
We can't do it for them,
Life isn't easy that way
We have to give them choices
Sit back and pray.

So I ask myself the question, do it over if I could?
And it's there I hear the answer, I don't think I would
Given the chance to do it over, I'd mess it all up again
I run the race differently and still wouldn't win

One day this earth will be a sheer memory
Cause the only time I will win
Is with God in Glory.

Hate

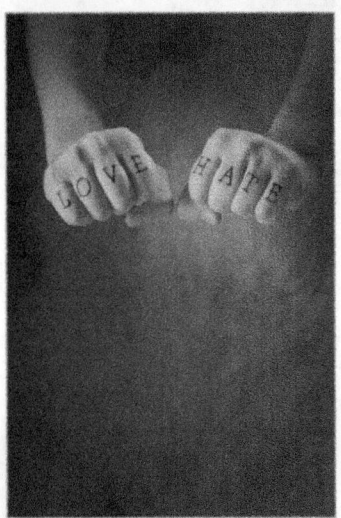

*"Rejoice with him, you heavens,
and let all of God's angels worship him.
Rejoice with his people, you Gentiles,
and let all the angels be strengthened in him.
For he will avenge the blood of his children;
he will take revenge against his enemies.
He will repay those who hate him and cleanse his people's land."
Deuteronomy 32:43*

Hate

Hate is a dark word
That strikes fear in our heart
Unfortunately, this world is full of it
And it is tearing us a part

It can cause the best of people
To make horrible choices it seems
It totally clouds your vision
Convincing people the end justifies their means

Hate is a powerful feeling
It takes control of your soul
It consumes you from the inside
And it doesn't want to let go

It's like a mighty sword
You sharpen with each hateful thought
Anticipating plunging that dagger
Often into blameless hearts

This feeling, it has killed many
Left victims from bombs, planes and towers
You see Satan is building his army
And the haters are his followers

There are more people abusing people
From tiny babies to our old
You can't even watch the news today
Without your insides growing cold

That's when I have to make the choice
And remind myself each day
That the end is drawing closer you see
And the enemy is ready to play

Choosing wisely my weapon
Will hold the key to my fate
I can choose to love like my Lord commanded
Or join the world and choose hate

I refuse to give into the enemy
I won't relinquish my power to him
You see my God has already got me
He is filling me up from within

Even when it takes every ounce of energy
To call upon His mighty name
He equips me with the strength I need
To beat Satan at his games

Which will you choose on that fateful day,
When the enemy is pushing you?
Will you hold steadfast to your beliefs?
Or will you let hate consume you?

Heart's Desire

*And I will give you a new heart,
and I will put a new spirit in you.
I will take out your stony, stubborn heart
and give you a tender, responsive heart.
Ezekiel 36:26*

Heart's Desire

There are things in life
I'll probably never understand
Like the desire to open our hearts
To the likes of mere man

We all want to be loved
Made to feel special, and adored
We so desire that extra touch
That leaves us longing for more

Even though we know the truth
That's hidden inside everyone's heart
There is going to come a day
That person will tear you apart

It may not be on purpose
But it will happen none the less
Because mere man is selfish
There is only so long it can be repressed

So what makes us desire it?
When we know it's only a matter of time
We get caught up in the emotions
Leaving us vulnerable and prime

Now don't get me wrong
I believe love does exist
But the feelings are so fleeting
Not sure they are worth the risk

It seems to take so long
For a broken heart to heal
Constantly picking up the pieces
Longing not to feel

Maybe my heart's desire
Needs to change its worldly focus
Look up and reach out to the one who is always there
The one who loves me, even when I'm broken

Scars

*For God called you to do good,
even if it means suffering,
just as Christ suffered for you.
1 Peter 2:21*

Scars

Sometimes when I am all alone
I feel so trapped inside
I have this hollow, aching feeling
and I just want to die

now don't take that to mean
I'm checking out on this world
it just means I'm struggling
Feeling Lost in other words

as I look back at my life
studying the paths that I've chose
not sure I would change things
it would make me a different person, I suppose

The Pain I have endured
etched deep inside of me
make me who I am today
like the scars upon a tree

No one else can see them
But I feel them every day
They Remind of where I've been
But also show me I've found my way

The days like this can take their toll
They threaten to lock me up, and bury my soul
Sometimes it's a war I'm not sure I can win
Somedays I'm a warrior and pick my shield up again

It's on those days when I decide to fight back
When I make the choice to not get off track
If I stay focused on those scars, that only I see
Then I'm giving them control, letting them define me

That's not a sacrifice that I'm willing to make
That is not why I was created, that is not my fate
I will not let the pain of this world take me down
I will struggle, and endure, and one day receive my crown

"Family"

For the son despises his father.
The daughter defies her mother.
The daughter-in-law defies her mother-in-law.
Your enemies are right in your own household!
As for me, I look to the LORD for help.
I wait confidently for God to save me,
and my God will certainly hear me.
Micah 7:6-7

"Family"

Blood family is one of those things
We unfortunately don't get to choose
Sometimes they are the easiest ones
To leave you battered or feeling bruised

Sometimes it's the cut of their tongue
That can just slice you in half
Sometimes it is their actions
You must force yourself to step back

Sometimes they have exhausted their chances
Taken way more than you had to take
Sometimes they are just plain selfish
Not caring who is at stake

Sometime they will pretend to care
Turn around and stab you in the back
But since they are supposed to be "Family"
It is very hard not to react

Hopefully you are a lucky one
Your family has always been there for you
If not, I pray you surround yourself
With "Family that YOU choose"

You see the one thing I can say
Throughout my years, I found it so very true
In times when my family have disappointed me
God placed others in my life to help me through

We were all born into a family
And they can help define who we are
But that doesn't mean we can't walk away
If they continue to break your heart

So I have learned to change my definition
Change what "Family" means to me
Now the only blood I let define me
Was the blood shed upon that tree

Giving Up

Trust in the LORD with all your heart;
do not depend on your own understanding.
Seek his will in all you do,
and he will show you which path to take.
Don't be impressed with your own wisdom.
Instead, fear the LORD and turn away from evil.
Then you will have healing for your body
and strength for your bones.
Proverbs 3:5-8

Giving Up

To some it might seem easier
To just give up and end their own life
If I'm gone who cares, they might say
They are just tired of the fight

For some, it may be because of their past
It's just more than they can bare
For others, it is their present
Not even realizing how they got there

No matter what the journey is
That brought them to this place
Their pain is so consuming now
They no longer search for His face

They might throw their fist up in anger
Or scream loudly into the air
But inside they have lost all hope a God
Will save them from their despair

I pray if you ever find yourself
One day standing at this place
That God will send an Angel to you
To show you, of His grace

These days ahead of you will quickly pass
Don't let the enemy lie to you
God promised never to leave your side
That IS the voice of truth

Our creator formed you for a purpose
Without your life, there would be a void
Your loved ones would be left behind
Their hearts would be destroyed

Getting through this season of time
May be the hardest thing you will ever have to do
God will give you the strength you need to endure
Only He can get you through

Pain

He comforts us in all our troubles so that we can comfort others. When they are troubled, we will be able to give them the same comfort God has given us. For the more we suffer for Christ, the more God will shower us with his comfort through Christ. Even when we are weighed down with troubles, it is for your comfort and salvation! For when we ourselves are comforted, we will certainly comfort you. Then you can patiently endure the same things we suffer.
2 Corinthians 1:4-6

Pain

Is there an emotion
That is different than the rest?
One that at times has controlled you
If you had to confess?

One that when it strikes, you feel it
No matter how big or strong you are
It can be as piercing as a bullet
Or just leave a tiny scar

It can have a very short life span
Leave as quickly as it came
Or it can seem to last forever
Leave you broken and forever changed

The wounds it leaves behind
May not always be seen
But the effects on your soul
Can make your heart want to scream

They have given this emotion a label
They have simply called it "Pain"
Sometimes it is so hard to handle
That you find someone else to blame

Some find themselves questioning everything'
Even if God really does exist
Satan will whisper in your ear
"Who would treat their child like this?"

If you believe the lies of Satan
Then he is the one who wins
He will use your pain to destroy you
Sending you places you have never been

The pain threatens to overtake you
Drawing you deeper into its grasp
It will consume you and make you miserable
Till you no longer care where you are at

However, there is someone who seeks to find you
You have never really been alone
But the pain can somehow blind you
Blurring the vision of God's mighty throne

He was there when you didn't feel Him
Because pain had turned you away
He didn't answer the prayer you desperately needed
So you felt angry and betrayed

As time goes on the pain goes much deeper
It will keep eating at your soul
Unless you choose to change it
Surrender, give it to God to control

You have held on to the pain so long
It's become a part of who you are
But God wants to grow you further
Not be defined by your painful scars

He never promised the road to be easy
We will suffer hardships along the way
But he does promise He will never leave you
Trust in Him, He won't lead you astray

Faith

"You don't have enough faith," Jesus told them.
"I tell you the truth, if you had faith even as small as a mustard seed,
you could say to this mountain,
'Move from here to there,' and it would move.
Nothing would be impossible."
Matthew 17:20

Faith

You have to remember
That all you need
Is faith as small
As a mustard seed

That's hard to see
When you feel, all hope is gone
But try falling to your knees
He will catch you if you call

In the end, when in heaven
There will be treasures awaiting you
But while we walk here on this earth
There will be many storms to suffer through

Just when you get that feeling
There is No one on your side
Remember what he did for you
That day, that He died

He is always there watching
He gave us free Will to choose
If you listen to the lies of Satan
You will be the one who will lose

God gave us His word
It is the only voice of truth
He has made us many promises
He will Never abandon you

You see that faith it grows daily
With each day that you let Him lead
Taking the weight off of your shoulders
He wants you to be freed

Each day will still be a struggle
Having that faith isn't always easy
Somedays it will be only that mustard seed
Somedays you will trust Him completely

On those days you give it all to Him
It will change you from within
The storms will still rage around you
But with faith, you will be comforted by Him

Surrendering it All

So the trouble is not with the law, for it is spiritual and good. The trouble is with me, for I am all too human, a slave to sin. I don't really understand myself, for I want to do what is right, but I don't do it. Instead, I do what I hate. But if I know that what I am doing is wrong, this shows that I agree that the law is good. So I am not the one doing wrong; it is sin living in me that does it.

And I know that nothing good lives in me, that is, in my sinful nature. I want to do what is right, but I can't. I want to do what is good, but I don't. I don't want to do what is wrong, but I do it anyway. But if I do what I don't want to do, I am not really the one doing wrong; it is sin living in me that does it.

I have discovered this principle of life—that when I want to do what is right, I inevitably do what is wrong. I love God's law with all my heart. But there is another power within me that is at war with my mind. This power makes me a slave to the sin that is still within me.
Romans 7:14-23

Surrendering it All

Ever stood in a crowded room,
Feeling hollow and completely alone?
Ever feel like the smile you put on,
Isn't really your own?

Ever feel like today will be just another day,
That you will be disappointed again?
Ever start dreaming of a better future,
Just to have the voices creep back in?

Ever just want to pack up and walk away,
Or somehow just get lost?
Ever want to just give up,
Stop caring what it might cost?

Ever want to stop believing,
That He is up there, and He cares?
Ever wonder where He was,
Or If He even hears my prayers?

Ever wonder what life might be like,
If you really did give in?
You see my friend I did this once,
But I Surrendered It All to Him

Ever wonder what that might look like,
Choosing to do this in your life?
Ever wondered if you would feel less burdened,
Letting God carry your strife?

Ever thought what the voices might sound like,
When replaced with the voice of truth?
Ever wondered what your heart might feel,
Knowing full well that He loves You?

Ever thought what people would look like,
Surrendering will give you new eyes to see.
Ever wondered why He would hang on that cross
He Surrendering It All first, for You and Me.

From the Author:

Thank you for Taking this time to read this book. Each Writing in this book was given to me, by God, through different phases of my life. Phases that we all seem to find ourselves in and sometimes cannot get out of. I pray that when you find yourself in one of these that you take this book back out and read that writing again. Let it encourage you that you are NEVER alone, and you can get to the other side. This book has been prayed over by a lot of people before it made it into your hands today and those will continue. I challenge you to 2 things.
First, Be a Light! Use any experience you have overcome, that had kept you in darkness, to help someone else. Second, Choose Love! This one needs no explanation, Just LOVE.

Dear Lord,
I come to you today and ask that you meet each Reader right where they are today. Let them feel your power and your Love so much that they cannot deny that they need you. I pray for our world and all it is facing in these ever-challenging times and that people always choose Love over Hate. Lord please let all who reads this feel you through it as these are your words not mine.
In Jesus Precious Name,
Amen

Be watching for more writings from Regina Thrasher coming soon.

For book signings and speaking engagements,
contact the author at:

Email   Regina@TravelsLikeRoyalty.com
Website   TravelsLikeRoyalty.com
Facebook   facebook.com/rthrasher2
LinkedIn   linkedin.com/in/regina-johnston-7ab2757

www.ingramcontent.com/pod-product-compliance
Lightning Source LLC
LaVergne TN
LVHW020058090426
835510LV00040B/2434